TOKYO DISNEY

Travel Guide 2025

Insider Tips, Hidden Gems and Money-Saving Secrets for Your Magical Japan Adventure

David M. Henson

© **Copyright (David M. Henson) 2025 - All rights reserved.**

The content contained within this book may not be reproduced, duplicated or transmitted without direct written permission from the author or the publisher.

Under no circumstances will any blame or legal responsibility be held against the publisher, or author, for any damages, reparation, or monetary loss due to the information contained within this book. Either directly or indirectly. You are responsible for your own choices, actions, and results.

Legal Notice:

This book is copyright protected. This book is only for personal use. You cannot amend, distribute, sell, use, quote or paraphrase any part, or the content within this book, without the consent of the author or publisher.

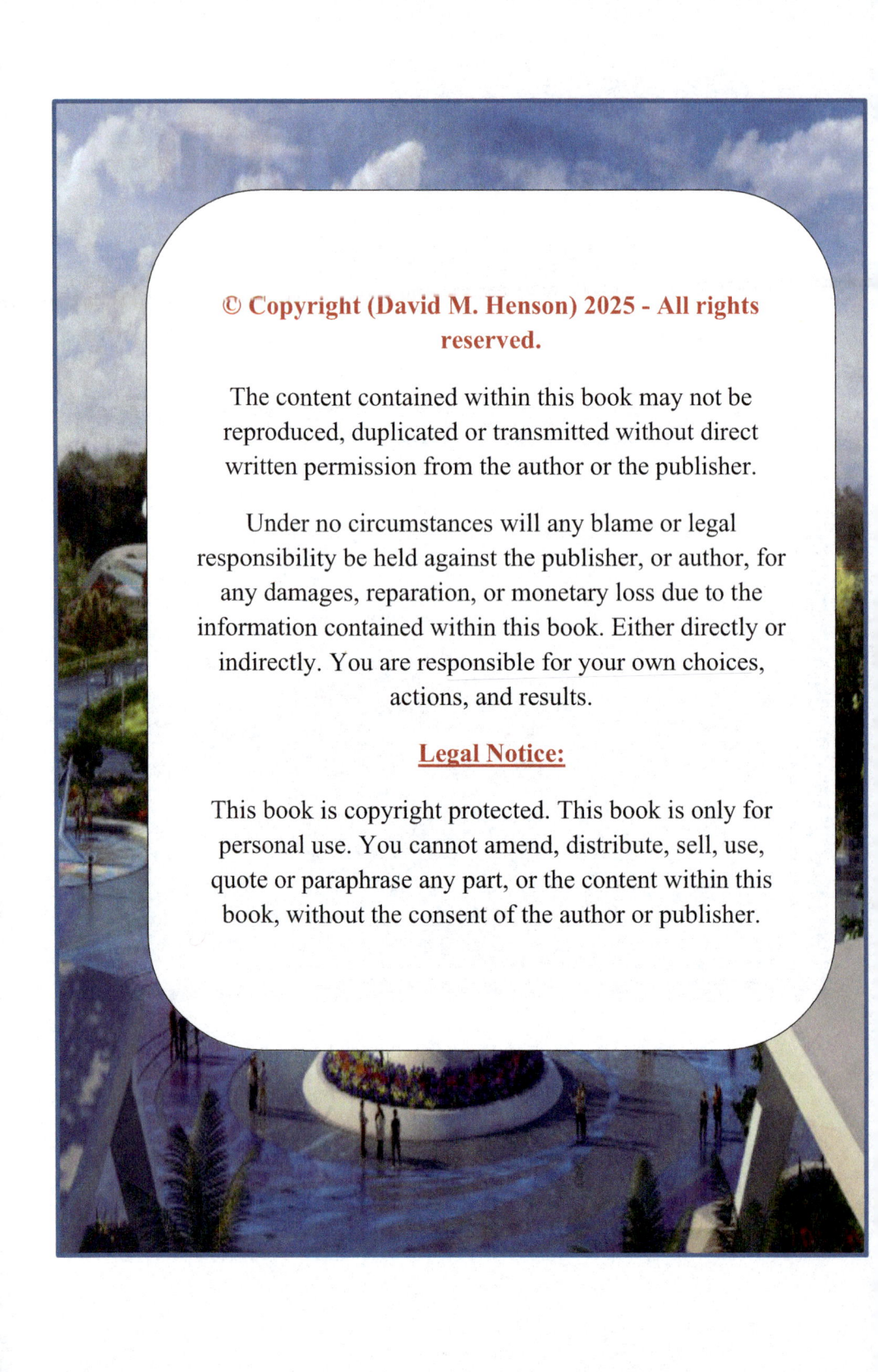

Dedication

This book is dedicated to all Disney enthusiasts, adventurers, and dreamers hoping to experience the wonder of Disneyland Tokyo. May this book be a reliable companion on your trip to one of the world's most stunning places? A special thank you to the dedicated cast members and surrounding communities who make Tokyo Disney Resort an exceptional place. Your enthusiasm and warmth permeate every page of this handbook. May your journey be full of joy, wonder, and amazing memories.

Disclaimer Notice

Please note the information contained within this document is for educational and entertainment purposes only. All effort has been executed to present accurate, up to date, and reliable, complete information. No warranties of any kind are declared or implied.

By reading this document, the reader agrees that under no circumstances is the author responsible for any losses, direct or indirect, which are incurred as a result of the use of the information contained within this document, including, but not limited to, — errors, omissions, or inaccuracies.

About The Author

David M. Henson is an accomplished travel writer and theme park expert specializing in Disney destinations worldwide. With over 15 years in travel journalism, Henson has established himself as a trusted authority for readers seeking comprehensive, practical guides to extraordinary places.

His fascination with Disney parks began in childhood, inspiring journeys to Disney resorts across the globe where he documented experiences and mastered the art of maximizing each visit. Henson's writing is distinguished by its thoroughness, blending insider knowledge with actionable advice for travellers of all types.

His expertise allows him to uncover hidden gems, must-experience attractions, and cultural nuances unique to each Disney destination. The Tokyo Disneyland Travel Guide 2025 emerges from his deep passion for Tokyo Disney Resort, offering readers expert navigation through this distinctive park.

Through meticulous research and multiple visits, Henson provides insights into everything from efficient itineraries to seasonal specialities, ensuring readers experience the magic of Tokyo Disneyland to its fullest potential.

TOKYO DISNEYLAND MAP

About The Book

Tokyo Disneyland Travel Guide 2025 is a comprehensive and current resource for anyone planning a visit to one of the world's most celebrated theme parks. This meticulously researched guide offers deep insights into the magical experience awaiting guests at Tokyo Disneyland, covering everything from must-see attractions, spectacular parades, and character encounters to the park's unique seasonal celebrations that transform the resort throughout the year.

Henson goes beyond standard attractions, sharing exclusive insider knowledge on optimal visiting times, efficient navigation strategies, and where to find the most exceptional dining options and memorable souvenirs. The guide thoughtfully explores the park's rich history, cultural nuances, and distinctive features that set Tokyo Disneyland apart from its global counterparts.

With detailed information on transportation options from central Tokyo and international airports, comprehensive accommodation reviews ranging from Disney hotels to budget-friendly alternatives, and expert advice on ticket purchasing strategies, this guide equips visitors to maximize every moment of their enchanting journey. Practical tips on FastPass utilization, language navigation, and culturally specific etiquette ensure a seamless experience.

Whether a first-time visitor or a seasoned Disney enthusiast, Travel Guide to Tokyo Disneyland 2025 is your essential companion for creating unforgettable memories in this uniquely Japanese interpretation of Disney magic.

Table of Contents

Introduction 7
    Brief History of Tokyo Disneyland. 8
    Why Visit Tokyo Disneyland in 2025? 8
    Important Facts and Practical Information 9

Top Attractions In Tokyo Disneyland 11
    Disneyland Park: The Heart of the Magic 11
    Tokyo Disneyland's Most Popular Theme Areas 13
    Tokyo DisneySea: The Unique Experience 15
    Parades and Live Performances .. 16

Hidden Gems At Tokyo Disneyland 17
    Secret Locations for Photography and Relaxation 17
    Lesser-Known Attractions to Visit 18
    Unique-Themed Experiences 19
    Quiet Corners for Peaceful Moments 20

What To Do And What Not To Do In Tokyo Disneyland 21
    What to Do 21
    What Not To Do 23

Itinerary For Different Types of Travelers 25
    One-Day Itinerary for First-Time Visitors 25
    One-Day Itinerary for Thrill Seekers 26
    One-Day Itinerary for Families with Young Children 27
    Weekend Itinerary for Relaxed Explorers 27
    Itinerary for Returning Visitors ... 28

Dining and Shopping at Tokyo Disneyland 29
    Must-Try Foods and Snacks 29
    Shopping For Souvenirs 30
    Dining Tips for Various Budgets .. 31

Seasonal Events and Special Experiences 33
    Tokyo Disneyland Seasonal Events 33
    Special Events in Tokyo Disneyland 35

Staying in Tokyo Disneyland 37
    Accommodation Options 37

What to Expect at Disney Hotels 39

Advantages of Staying On-site 40

Tips for Booking Your Stay 40

Tips and Recommendations for a Smooth Visit 41

Maximising Your Visit.................. 41

Essential Packing List................... 43

Making the Most of Your Stay 43

Nearby Attractions & Day Trips 45

Exploring Tokyo and Beyond....... 45

Exploring Disney Resort's Other Parks.. 47

Shopping and Dining in Tokyo..... 47

Insider Tips and Personalized Travel Plans 49

Visitor Reviews and Testimonials 49

Exclusive Tips from Disney Experts 50

Planning Tips for Solo Travelers .. 51

Celebrations and Special Occasions at Tokyo Disneyland..................... 51

Personalized Itinerary Suggestions 52

Practical Information and Sustainable Travel......................... 53

Budget Travel Guide 53

Behind the Scenes at Tokyo Disneyland 54

Health and Safety Tips 55

Cultural Etiquette for Visiting Tokyo Disneyland........................ 56

Weather Guide and Best Time to Visit 56

Sustainable Travel Tips 57

Detailed Map and Photography Guide 59

How to Use QR Code Maps.......... 59

Best Places for Photography........ 61

Appendix..................................... 67

Useful Apps for Tokyo Disneyland 67

Useful Websites 67

Emergency Contacts 68

FAQs.. 68

Conclusion 69

Glossary of Terms 70

INTRODUCTION

Tokyo Disneyland is nothing short of a fantastic realm where Disney's charm meets Japanese creativity and efficiency. Millions visit this famous park in Urayasu, Chiba, just a short distance from Tokyo's core every year. The park offers the ideal combination of nostalgic Disney classics and exciting new attractions, guaranteeing that first-time guests and returning fans leave with unforgettable experiences. Unlike many Disney parks worldwide, Tokyo Disneyland stands out not just for its breathtaking attractions and characters but also for its meticulous attention to detail and superb service. Whether you're a toddler discovering Mickey Mouse for the first time or an adult revisiting childhood memories, Tokyo Disneyland offers a fantastic escape into fantasy. It has seven themed lands: Adventureland, Fantasyland, Tomorrowland, Westernland, Critter Country, Toontown, and World Bazaar, all painstakingly crafted to immerse guests in different Disney storylines.

Brief History of Tokyo Disneyland

The goal of opening a Disney Park in Japan was realized in 1983 when Tokyo Disneyland became the first Disney Park outside the United States. It resulted from a collaboration between The Walt Disney Company and the Oriental Land Company. Unlike other overseas Disney parks, Tokyo Disneyland's design is strongly influenced by Disneyland in Anaheim, California, but it stands out for its layout, cultural features, and attention to detail.

The park has grown and changed over the years, with new attractions such as Pooh's Hunny Hunt, a ground-breaking ride that employs cutting-edge technology to provide a one-of-a-kind experience each time. Today, Tokyo Disneyland is one of the world's most popular theme parks, renowned for its friendliness, attention to detail, and immersive atmosphere.

Why Visit Tokyo Disneyland in 2025?

2025 promises to be a fantastic year for visiting Tokyo Disneyland. With the park's continued efforts to improve existing attractions, offer seasonal events, and develop new experiences, 2025 will be jam-packed with new and thrilling adventures for guests of all ages. Expect fresh entertainment acts, rides, and seasonal activities to keep the enchantment alive and surprise guests.

Whether you want to experience the newest attractions, such as the highly anticipated "Beauty and the Beast" themed section, or rediscover timeless classics, Tokyo Disneyland has something for everyone. For Disney fans, the park's dedication to keeping its original charm while adding modern technology makes the experience unique. And for guests who last came a while ago, 2025 will provide new sights and sensations that will make you feel like you're visiting a new park.

Important Facts and Practical Information
Where and How to Get There

Tokyo Disneyland is located in Urayasu, Chiba, Japan, approximately 30 minutes from central Tokyo. The precise address is:

Tokyo Disneyland: 1-1 Maihama, Urayasu, Chiba 279-0031, Japan.
Geographic coordinates: 35.6322°N, 139.8804°E.

To reach there, take the JR Keiyo Line from Tokyo Station to Maihama Station (about 15 minutes). The park entrance is only a short walk from Maihama Station, or you may use the Disney Resort Line, a monorail that connects the park to neighboring hotels and commercial centers.

If you're staying in Tokyo, the park is easily accessible by public transportation. The Resort Line offers a delightful, picturesque journey around the whole resort region.

Opening Hours and Calendar

Tokyo Disneyland is open year-round, with different hours based on the season, day of the week, and special events. The park typically opens between 8:00 and 10:00 a.m. and closes between 9:00 and 11:00 p.m.

During peak seasons, such as summer vacation, Christmas, and spring break, the park is open longer to accommodate more customers. It's always a good idea to check the official Tokyo Disneyland website for the most up-to-date hours, especially if planning a trip around special events or holidays.

Tickets and Prices

Ticket rates for Tokyo Disneyland vary depending on the season and if you want to visit Tokyo Disneyland or Tokyo DisneySea (the sister park). A one-day adult ticket for ages 12 and up typically costs roughly ¥7,400 (around USD 70). Multi-day tickets and Park Hopper passes enable you to visit both parks on the same day and are also available for a slightly higher fee.

Tickets may be purchased online through the official Tokyo Disneyland website or from approved ticket dealers in Japan. International tourists should obtain tickets in advance to avoid extensive waits at the entry.

Park Rules and Guidelines

Before entering the park, it is essential to understand its rules and procedures to guarantee a smooth and pleasurable stay. Here are some critical factors to bear in mind.

Bags & Items: Large bags, coolers, and alcoholic beverages are prohibited. Only small luggage and personal belongings should be taken inside.

Smoking is permitted only in designated smoking locations throughout the park.

Prohibited Items: Drones, giant umbrellas, and dogs (except service animals) are prohibited in the park.

Photography: While photography is encouraged, most places do not permit flash photography and selfie sticks.

Adhere to the park's laws and regulations to ensure a safe and enjoyable experience for yourself and other visitors.

Tokyo Disneyland is where dreams come true, combining fun, nostalgia, and adventure into one unforgettable location. Whether you're a first-time visitor or a seasoned Disney fan, the park provides limitless pleasure. The following chapters of this book will take you deep into the top attractions, insider insights, and everything else you'll need to make the most of your 2025 Tokyo Disneyland trip.

TOP ATTRACTIONS IN TOKYO DISNEYLAND

Tokyo Disneyland is a realm of endless adventure and nostalgia, with something for everyone, whether you're a thrill-seeker, a Disney fan, or just seeking a pleasant day with family and friends. After spending several days visiting the park, I can confidently declare that the top attractions are the core of the magic. Tokyo Disneyland ensures a fantastic experience with timeless Disney classics, exhilarating rides, and dazzling live performances.

Disneyland Park: The Heart of the Magic

Tokyo Disneyland is divided into many themed regions, each with its own distinct charm. Disneyland Park, home to some of the park's most renowned attractions, is the major center of activity.

Splash Mountain

Splash Mountain, located in Westernland, is a must-see attraction for all visitors. This log flume attraction features catchy music, lovely animatronics, and a spectacular final plunge. Based on Disney's Song of the South relates the narrative of Br'er Rabbit and his travels in the bayou. The twist occurs when you take the drop at the conclusion, making this an ideal ride for people looking for fun and thrill. It's also one of the finest ways to cool yourself on a hot day, so expect to get a bit wet!

Pirates of the Caribbean

This popular ride in Adventureland is a must-see for Disney enthusiasts. Traveling through the dark, pirate-infested waterways, you'll come across compelling sights and fantastic animatronic pirates. The sights, sounds, and fragrances bring the Caribbean ambiance to life, from pirates' rum-soaked antics to stranded treasures. The ride is both eerie and entertaining, suitable for people of all ages, and an excellent opportunity to escape the park's crowds.

Space Mountain

Space Mountain is one of the most thrilling rides at Tokyo Disneyland.

This indoor rollercoaster propels you through the universe with twists, turns, and severe drops—all in complete darkness. The futuristic atmosphere, replete with starry sky and high-speed thrills, makes it a favorite destination for travelers seeking excitement. The ride is ideal for individuals who appreciate roller coasters with a sci-fi theme.

Big Thunder Mountain

Every vacation to Disneyland is complete with a ride on Big Thunder Mountain, the most thrilling ride in the forest. Located in Westernland, this high-speed rollercoaster takes you through an ancient mine where the track appears to be breaking apart. The twists are sharp, and the unexpected dips take you by surprise. The theming is immersive, and the exhilarating ride experience and the park's picturesque surroundings make this attraction a must-see for all visitors.

Tokyo Disneyland's Most Popular Theme Areas

Each themed section at Tokyo Disneyland has its special magic, allowing guests to explore diverse worlds and stories from the Disney realm.

Tomorrowland

When you enter Tomorrowland, you will feel like you have been transported into the future. This section has some of the park's most futuristic attractions, such as Space Mountain, Buzz Lightyear's Astro Blasters, and the entertaining Monsters, Inc. Ride and Seek. The sleek design, high-tech gadgets, and neon lighting create a distinctly modern ambiance, and the rides are ideal for people seeking action-packed entertainment.

Fantasy Land

Fantasyland is the core of Tokyo Disneyland, bringing the fantasy of great Disney films to life. You may enter Cinderella Castle, the park's famous centerpiece, and see popular attractions like Peter Pan's Flight, It's a Small World, and The Many Adventures of Winnie the Pooh. The fairy-tale appeal of this region takes visitors to a realm of dreams, where each corner has a fresh narrative waiting to be told.

Adventureland

Adventureland combines adventure and entertainment. This place offers an experience for the entire family, whether you're sailing through the jungle-on-Jungle Cruise, getting lost in the wild West on Big Thunder Mountain, or living out your swashbuckling pirate fantasies on Pirates of the Caribbean. The theming is rich in storytelling, resulting in an immersive experience that takes visitors to other worlds.

Critter Country

Critter Country is a must-see for lovers of Winnie the Pooh and his many adventures. You may join Pooh and his buddies as they trek around the Hundred Acre Wood. The lovely surroundings, rich flora, and whimsical design make this location feel like a storybook come to life. Visit neighboring Splash Mountain for a blend of thrills and fun!

Tokyo DisneySea: The Unique Experience

Tokyo DisneySea, next to Tokyo Disneyland, provides an entirely different experience with its maritime atmosphere and thrilling attractions. It's a hidden gem you shouldn't miss, especially if you're a Disney lover seeking something different.

The Venetian Gondola Ride

The Venetian Gondola Ride is one of DisneySea's most romantic and calm attractions. Located in Mediterranean Harbor, this trip allows you to lean back and relax as a gondolier guides you through the lovely canals, passing past spectacular Venetian-style buildings. The environment is tranquil, and the vista is breathtaking—ideal for couples or anybody looking for a relaxing break from the more intense attractions.

Journey to the Center of the Earth

Journey to the Center of the Earth, situated on Mysterious Island, is an exciting, high-tech attraction that takes you deep beneath. Inspired by Jules Verne's classic, this trip mixes incredible storytelling, jaw-dropping sights, and surprising turns. The voyage concludes with a heart-pounding conclusion that will have you on the edge of your seats.

Tower of Terror

Tower of Terror is an absolute must-ride for adrenaline seekers. This drop ride in American Waterfront takes you on a thrilling tour through an abandoned hotel where a cursed treasure awaits. The ride's theming is detailed, and the surprising drops keep you returning for more.

Twenty Thousand Leagues under the Sea

This undersea journey on Mysterious Island allows you to explore the ocean's depths and discover aquatic animals and mysteries. The experience is visually striking, blending technology and imagination to bring you to the heart of the sea. It's an unforgettable, engaging event that should not be missed.

Parades and Live Performances

Tokyo Disneyland excels not just in rides but also in live entertainment. The parades and displays are an essential component of the event.

Dreaming Up! Parade

Dreaming Up! is a must-see for any tourist. The Parade is a colorful show featuring Disney characters, floats, and music. It's a lovely way to experience Disney's enchantment while watching iconic characters come to life right before you.

Seasonal shows and performances

Tokyo Disneyland hosts seasonal shows and performances all year long. Whether it's Halloween, Christmas, or a summer event, there's always something new to discover. These exceptional events showcase one-of-a-kind personalities, lavish costumes, and breathtaking sights that commemorate the changing seasons.

HIDDEN GEMS AT TOKYO DISNEYLAND

Tokyo Disneyland is a magical location, but there are hidden gems that many tourists miss out on. These hidden jewels provide a one-of-a-kind and relaxing way to experience the park's enchantment. Whether you're looking for a peaceful location to unwind, an off-the-beaten-path attraction, or a unique picture opportunity, Tokyo Disneyland offers many surprises. Allow me to lead you on a tour through these lesser-known jewels.

Secret Locations for Photography and Relaxation

While Tokyo Disneyland's big attractions are a photographer's dream, there are hidden gems around the park that allow you to capture a more intimate or distinctive aspect of the excitement. One of my faves is the serene Mickey's Toontown. Nestled in the rear of the park, this quirky, vivid region feels almost mysterious, with colorful houses and a humorous atmosphere. It's an ideal location for photographs, particularly near Goofy's Bounce House, where the fanciful constructions provide a bright, energetic backdrop.

If you want to escape it all, visit Fantasyland and visit the beautiful Alice's Tea Party area. This delightful area, complete with gigantic teacups and Alice-themed decor, is ideal for people-watching. The soothing hues and inventive design provide a relaxing ambiance suitable for recharging.

Lesser-Known Attractions to Visit

While everyone goes to Space Mountain and Pirates of the Caribbean, Tokyo Disneyland offers a few less busy rides but just as impressive.

The Enchanted Tiki Room

The Enchanted Tiki Room, hidden away in Adventureland, is a classic Disney attraction that many people overlook, but it's a fantastic spot to experience Disney's charm in a new manner. Inside the Tiki Room, you'll be surrounded by colorful tropical flowers and animated birds singing delightful songs. The program is ageless, and its old-school charm never fails to make me grin. It's also a terrific spot to escape the crowd for a while, with the indoor atmosphere providing a nice respite from the heat.

Westernland Shooting Gallery

Located in Westernland, this hidden gem provides an old-school shooting experience. It's easy to go right past it without noticing, but if you take the time to stop, you'll be rewarded with an enjoyable and participatory experience. Armed with a toy rifle, you may aim at various targets and enjoy the thrill of striking a moving object. It's a throwback to the Wild West and a terrific, low-key attraction with short wait times.

Unique-Themed Experiences

For those searching for anything other than the standard Disney attractions, Tokyo Disneyland has a few unique, specialized experiences that are nothing short of remarkable.

Club 33: An Exclusive Dining Experience

Club 33, a members-only restaurant in Adventureland's New Orleans Square, is one of the park's most secretive locations. This exclusive club is rooted in Disney heritage and represents the pinnacle of luxury. Club 33 has minimal access; only members and guests can dine there. The atmosphere is exquisite and full of Disney's trademark charm, and the cuisine matches any high-end restaurant in town. While it's out of reach for most visitors, there's something unique about knowing that such a private area exists within the park, discreetly providing the ultimate Disney experience.

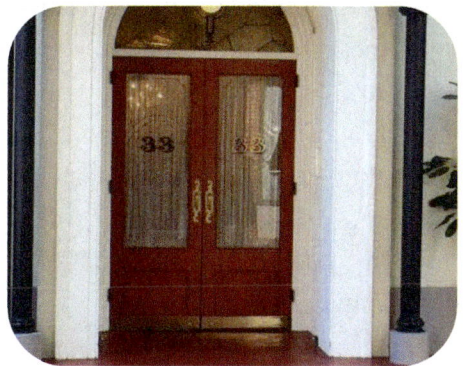

The Magical World of Ghibli Exhibition

Fans of Studio Ghibli will enjoy an immersive experience at Tokyo Disneyland's Magical World of Ghibli Exhibition, located in Tomorrowland. While not precisely inside Disneyland, it is a short walk from Ikspiari, the park's nearby shopping area. This exhibition highlights the extraordinary creativity and animation that have made Ghibli films famous worldwide. It's an unassuming jewel for everyone who likes Hayao Miyazaki's fascinating worlds. The attention to detail in the exhibits, together with the enchanting aura, make this a must-see for Ghibli fans.

Quiet Corners for Peaceful Moments

Amid Tokyo Disneyland's bustle and vitality, you sometimes need a quiet area to rest and recharge. Fortunately, the park has various hidden corners for relaxation and tranquility.

One such location is the Secret Garden in Fantasyland, hidden behind the famed Cinderella Castle. This lovely, well-kept garden provides a peaceful retreat from the crowd, with magnificent flowers, ivy-covered walls, and the calm murmur of fountains. It's a nice area to relax, get a snack, or watch the world go by. Another serene site is near the Pirates of the Caribbean attraction, where there is a quiet promenade with shaded chairs, ideal for a moment of relaxation in a less-trafficked park area.

A peaceful trail through Critter Country leads to Splash Mountain if you want to go further. This walk, surrounded by beautiful trees and the soothing sounds of water, feels like a hidden treasure. It's an excellent way to escape the crowd, especially if you want to take a leisurely walk and appreciate the beauty at your own pace.

Tokyo Disneyland is a place of discovery. Although the big attractions are undoubtedly worth seeing, these hidden jewels provide a calmer, more intimate peek into the park's charm. Whether you're searching for a quiet getaway, an engaging experience, or a taste of Disney's distinct charm, these hidden gems will make your vacation unforgettable.

WHAT TO DO AND WHAT NOT TO DO IN TOKYO DISNEYLAND

Tokyo Disneyland is a lovely location, but to make the most of your visit, keep a few things in mind. After spending a significant amount of time touring the park, I've discovered that a good Disneyland trip requires a combination of planning, strategy, and flexibility. Here's what you should do (and avoid) to make your stay as enjoyable and stress-free as possible.

What to Do
Use the Disney FastPass System
One of the most significant ways to make the most of your time at Tokyo Disneyland is to use the Disney FastPass system. This free service allows you to book entry to several of the park's most popular attractions, which can help you avoid excessive waits. My advice? Start early and go to the FastPass distribution spots as soon as the park opens. Attractions like Splash

useful tool for exploring the park's offerings.

Stay Hydrated and Take Breaks

Tokyo Disneyland may get hot and busy, particularly during peak seasons, so remain hydrated and rest frequently. It's easy to get caught up in the excitement, but I discovered the hard way that pacing oneself is essential. I recommend having a refillable water bottle and refilling it at one of the many water stations distributed throughout the park. The paths are lined with covered areas where you may rest and relax, providing an ideal time to refuel.

There's also something relaxing about being away from the masses, even for a few minutes. For a little break from the crowds, consider visiting Fantasyland or the Secret Garden behind Cinderella Castle.

Mountain and Pirates of the Caribbean are frequently in great demand, so getting a FastPass might save you time and let you explore other park areas.

I highly recommend downloading the Disneyland App (available for iOS and Android) to keep track of which rides offer FastPasses and available hours. This app is a very

Take advantage of seasonal and themed events

Tokyo Disneyland is renowned for its ever-changing seasonal and themed events. Each event adds charm to your stay, whether it's the eerie Halloween festivities or the bright Christmas celebrations. If you're visiting during one of these periods, check the event schedule and arrange your itinerary accordingly.

Special parades, themed products, and limited-time attractions make these times essential to the Disneyland experience. Look for unique menus and rare goods that appear during these events!

Check the Disneyland app for wait times

The Disneyland App is a must-have throughout your vacation. It offers real-time updates on wait times, showtimes, parade timetables, and food options. It allows you to arrange your day better, avoid long lineups, and find hidden treasures that might otherwise go unnoticed. Remember to look for special discounts or events during your visit. Tokyo Disneyland frequently offers limited-time specials and experiences to make your day even more spectacular.

What Not To Do

Do not ignore safety instructions on rides

It's tempting to become enthusiastic and rush into rides without paying close attention to safety precautions, but I strongly advise listening attentively. Not only is it necessary for your safety, but the instructions are sometimes brilliantly integrated into the ride's tale. For example, on Space Mountain, the pre-ride movie provides vital safety information colorfully and engagingly.

Avoid overpacking and go light

Spending the entire day in the park makes it easy to overpack. However, carrying too much weight will prevent you from slowing down. I recommend bringing only the essentials: sunscreen, a light jacket, and a camera or phone for photography. Lockers are accessible at the park if you need to store additional belongings, but it's better to travel light and simple.

Remember sunscreen

The Tokyo sun may be surprisingly powerful, particularly during the summer months. While it may seem incredible in the morning, the sun may damage your skin during the day. Trust me, it's easy to forget sunscreen while having fun, but I always recommend applying it in the morning and reapplying throughout the day. The Sunshine Plaza and outdoor waiting lines might expose you to direct sunlight for an extended time.

Remember to catch the parades and shows

I understand that many tourists focus mainly on the attractions, but you should take advantage of the parades and live entertainment at Tokyo Disneyland. These performances are a key component of the Disney experience. From the breathtaking Dreaming Up! Parade to the magical Disney on Parade! The parades bring Disney's enchantment to life in ways that the attractions alone cannot. Make sure to verify showtimes ahead of time and schedule these events into your itinerary.

Only visit during peak times with prior planning

Tokyo Disneyland may get busy during peak holidays or school vacation periods. Additional planning goes a long way if you intend to travel during these periods. Arrive early to avoid crowds, and watch the app for wait time updates. ScheduleSchedule your visit during off-peak hours for a more relaxing experience.

Following these easy suggestions will allow you to make the most of your stay at Tokyo Disneyland. The magic surrounds you, but a little forethought may enhance your experience. Whether using FastPasses, staying hydrated, or discovering hidden treasures, there's no reason your Disneyland vacation shouldn't be spectacular!

ITINERARY FOR DIFFERENT TYPES OF TRAVELERS

Tokyo Disneyland is a beautiful site that can accommodate all types of guests, whether it's your first visit or you're returning for another round of enchantment. After several visits, I've discovered that a well-planned schedule is essential for a successful experience. In this chapter, I'll detail itinerary options for various tourists, ensuring everyone gets the most out of their day.

One-Day Itinerary for First-Time Visitors

If this is your first visit to Tokyo Disneyland, you'll want to soak in the park's renowned enchantment while visiting all the key attractions. This one-day plan will help you tour the park quickly and ensure you see all the must-see attractions.

Top Attractions to Prioritize

Begin your day by visiting Pirates of the Caribbean in Adventureland (address 1-1 Maihama, Urayasu, Chiba 279-0031, Japan). This realistic boat ride through pirate-infested waterways is one of the park's most popular attractions and should be on your list. Afterward, head to Critter Country's Splash Mountain for an exciting log-flume ride before getting wet—ideal for a warm day!

By mid-morning, travel to Space Mountain in Tomorrowland for some high-speed extraterrestrial adventure. If time permits, visit Big Thunder Mountain in Westernland, a roller coaster that promises a thrilling trip through the thrilling West.

Best Shows and Parades to Watch

Make sure to check the schedule for The Dreaming Up! The Parade takes place in the afternoon. Find a location near World Bazaar to get the best view of this fantastic spectacle as Disney characters come to life in glittering costumes and floats. Take advantage of the Disneyland Nighttime Parade, a visual feast of lights, music, and all your favorite characters.

One-Day Itinerary for Thrill Seekers

Tokyo Disneyland has many adrenaline-pumping rides for those who thrive on them. This schedule is ideal for adrenaline seekers looking to make the most of a high-energy day.

Top Roller Coasters & Thrill Rides

Start your day with a visit to Space Mountain, where you may experience incredible speed and thrills. Then, proceed to Big Thunder Mountain, where the most thrilling roller coaster ride in Westernland awaits. After that, take on the Splash Mountain rollercoaster, which ends with a spectacular plummet.

For a genuinely exhilarating experience, don't miss Journey to the Center of the Earth at Tokyo DisneySea. This journey has breathtaking views and high-speed dips that will have you on the edge of your seat.

How to Maximize Time on High-Energy Attractions

To make the most of your day, use the Disney FastPass system. This allows you to bypass standard lines and get right to the action. Start your day early and prioritize the most popular thrill rides, as lines are longer during the day.

One-Day Itinerary for Families with Young Children

If you're traveling with young children, Tokyo Disneyland is an absolute dream with its family-friendly rides and interactive attractions. This schedule is geared toward families searching for fun and relaxation.

Child-Friendly Rides and Attractions

Begin the day with a trip to Fantasyland, where your children may take a wonderful boat ride on It's a Small World. Then, they can enjoy the gentle thrill of The Many Adventures of Winnie the Pooh. Mickey's Toontown is another excellent destination where children can explore and engage with characters such as Mickey and Minnie.

Top Family Dining Spots

For lunch, visit Plaza Restaurant (near World Bazaar), which serves a mix of Western and Japanese cuisine in a family-friendly setting. Alternatively, Crystal Palace Restaurant in Fantasyland offers a sumptuous buffet with character encounters to amuse your children throughout dinner.

Relaxing and Interactive Activities for Children

After lunch, head to the Enchanted Tiki Room for a relaxing but engaging musical presentation. Take a break by meandering around the Secret Garden, a hidden gem near Cinderella Castle that provides a peaceful setting for children to explore while they relax.

Weekend Itinerary for Relaxed Explorers

If you have more time and prefer a slower pace, a weekend schedule allows you to appreciate the park more calmly and unhurriedly.

A mix of relaxing, scenic, and fun attractions

Begin the day by visiting Critter Country and enjoying the beautiful Splash Mountain before going to Fantasyland. After that, stroll around the park's gardens before stopping by the picturesque Westernland for a serene train ride on the Western River Railroad.

On day two, head to Tokyo DisneySea, where you may enjoy a picturesque gondola ride through the Mediterranean Harbor or explore the deep depths of 20,000 Leagues Under the Sea.

Hidden Gems for a Quiet Retreat

Take some time to unwind at The Magic Lamp Theater on the Arabian Coast, one of the park's calmer locations, where you can escape the crowd and enjoy a delightful show. These hidden jewels are ideal for people who want to soak in the park's beauty without feeling rushed.

Itinerary for Returning Visitors

If you've already been to Tokyo Disneyland, there are still many new things to explore, including seasonal events and newly introduced attractions.

Discovering New Attractions

Begin by touring the New Tomorrowland or taking in any new limited-time exhibits or parades. Tokyo Disneyland is constantly growing, so even repeat visitors may enjoy a new experience.

Special Experiences and Events

Finally, reserve a meal experience at Club 33, the private members-only club, for a taste of pure Disney luxury. You'll go away with recollections of an extraordinary, one-of-a-kind event.

These different itineraries will allow you to make the most of your visit to Tokyo Disneyland, regardless of your interests or speed. Tokyo Disneyland has something for everyone, from thrilling rides to relaxing getaways, making it an ideal location for all travelers.

DINING AND SHOPPING AT TOKYO DISNEYLAND

One of the most enjoyable features of any Tokyo Disneyland trip is the variety of food and shopping options available. Whether you're enjoying one of the park's wonderfully themed meals or looking for the ideal gift to take home, the park excels at transforming even the most ordinary activities into spectacular experiences. After multiple visits, I've gotten familiar with the greatest places to dine and buy, and I'm eager to share them with you.

Must-Try Foods and Snacks

Tokyo Disneyland is famous for its attractions, but it is also a food heaven. From savory appetizers to sweet treats, the food here will leave you wanting more.

Popcorn Flavors Exclusive to Disneyland

Popcorn may appear to be a simple snack, but at Tokyo Disneyland, it is a whole experience. You'll find a variety of cuisines throughout the park, many of which are unique to Tokyo Disneyland. My favorite is the Salted Caramel Popcorn in Adventureland (35.6329° N, 139.8804° E). It's rich and sweet without being too sugary, and the bags are the perfect size for snacking while visiting the park.

Other varieties include Honey and Soy Sauce, which goes well with the park's Japanese cuisine, and Curry Popcorn, which has a spicy, savory touch. These popcorn carts are more than simply locations to get a snack; each cart is themed to match the neighborhood. Whether visiting Tomorrowland or meandering through Fantasyland, bring a bag from one of these bright, quirky kiosks.

Meals in Themed Restaurants

For a more substantial lunch, Tokyo Disneyland's themed restaurants include a range of alternatives that will keep you full and happy. If you want Japanese food, head to Restaurant Hokusai in Tomorrowland (coordinates: 35.6333° N, 139.8807° E). The restaurant, which serves sushi, tempura, and bento boxes, provides a tranquil, elegant atmosphere to recuperate after a day of activity.

For a more fanciful experience, visit the Crystal Palace Restaurant in Fantasyland. This buffet-style restaurant is well-known for its character dining, where popular Disney characters, including Winnie the Pooh and Tigger, accompany you. It's an excellent place for families to unwind and eat a full supper (coordinates: 35.6306° N, 139.8805° E).

Shopping For Souvenirs

Every trip to Tokyo Disneyland is complete with collecting some

Disney-themed souvenirs. The shopping experience here is fantastic, with something for everyone, from soft toys to unique Disney items.

Disney Merchandise and Limited-Edition Items

Tokyo Disneyland is well-known for its limited-edition products, and if you're a collector, you'll want to visit the World Bazaar (coordinates 35.6328° N, 139.8806° E). You'll find a variety of one-of-a-kind and seasonal things that can't be found anywhere else. Watch out for exclusive pins, clothes, and limited-edition plush toys commemorating specific seasons or anniversaries.

For a more refined experience, the Disney Fantasy Shop in Fantasyland provides elegant goods ranging from Disney-inspired jewelry to finely created home furnishings. It's an excellent spot to buy something unique to commemorate your vacation.

Top Shops for Themed Souvenirs

If you're seeking gifts that will remind you of the wonder of Tokyo Disneyland long after you've left, I recommend stopping at The Emporium, just outside the entrance of World Bazaar (35.6331° N, 139.8807° E). This massive store sells everything from Mickey Mouse ears to themed apparel, toys, and memorabilia. It's one of the park's larger stores, and you could easily spend a few hours perusing the selection of products on exhibit.

Remember to visit Gag Factory in Toontown (35.6318° N, 139.8809° E). This charming boutique sells amusing Disney items such as novelty items, T-shirts, and character-themed items that will make you grin.

Dining Tips for Various Budgets

Tokyo Disneyland provides something for everyone, whether you're on a tight budget or searching for a luxury dining experience.

Cost-effective Meal Options

If you want to save money, there are many tasty, low-cost alternatives around the park. Cotton Top Café in Westernland (coordinates: 35.6313° N, 139.8787° E) serves affordable sandwiches, snacks, and cooked dinners in a friendly, rural atmosphere. Another fantastic alternative is The fantastic American Waffle Co. (coordinates: 35.6325° N, 139.8813° E) near World Bazaar, which serves freshly prepared waffles topped with fruit, whipped cream, or even savory options such as sausage or cheese.

Fine Dining Experiences

If you want something more premium, Tokyo Disneyland offers a variety of fine dining options. Blue Bayou Restaurant at Adventureland (coordinates: 35.6320° N, 139.8814° E) is an excellent choice for a romantic evening. A delicious lunch may be enjoyed within the Pirates of the Caribbean rollercoaster while watching boats float by. The environment here is very immersive, with the soft glow of lanterns and the sound of water providing a wonderful dining experience.

Treat yourself to lunch at Club 33, an elite members-only restaurant that requires advanced reservations. This restaurant in Adventureland serves excellent cuisine with a touch of Disney exclusivity—though gaining entrance may require some insider information!

Tokyo Disneyland is as much about dining and shopping as it is about thrills. Everything seems excellent, whether indulging in unique popcorn tastes, shopping for one-of-a-kind Disney souvenirs, or dining in a themed restaurant. With a little organization and a spirit of adventure, you can make the most of these opportunities and bring home memories that will last a lifetime.

SEASONAL EVENTS AND SPECIAL EXPERIENCES

One of the most charming features of visiting Tokyo Disneyland is the park's seasonal transformations throughout the year. Each season provides its own set of extraordinary events, parades, and unique shows that add a new level of excitement to your visit. As a frequent visitor who has visited Tokyo Disneyland during different seasons, I can attest that the park's ability to immerse you in the excitement of each celebration is unrivaled. Let me walk you through some of Tokyo Disneyland's most memorable seasonal events and exceptional experiences.

Tokyo Disneyland Seasonal Events

Halloween Events and Themed Rides

Tokyo Disneyland's Halloween events are among the most entertaining and creative. Every year, the park transforms into a frightening wonderland with elaborate decorations, themed rides, and Halloween-themed events. From late September to October, guests may enjoy a unique combination of fun scares and family-friendly thrills.

The Haunted Mansion Holiday (coordinates 35.6306° N, 139.8805° E) is a must-see during Halloween. This seasonal version of the popular Haunted Mansion ride features spooky yet lovely décor inspired by The Nightmare Before Christmas. Imagine being swept away in a haunted elevator, surrounded by wicked figures like Jack Skellington and Sally, all while creepy Halloween music fills the air. It combines eerie and cheerful elements, making it ideal for thrill seekers as well as families with small children.

Aside from the attractions, Tokyo Disneyland offers unique Halloween products, including Mickey and Minnie costumes, frightening snacks, and seasonally inspired home décor. As you go around the park, you'll see picture possibilities at every turn, whether it's a pumpkin farm or a larger-than-life Mickey Mouse pumpkin near the entrance to World Bazaar (coordinates: 35.6331° N, 139.8807° E). These seasonal festivities make Halloween a special occasion.

Christmas Parades & Shows

When December rolls around, Tokyo Disneyland transforms into a winter paradise. The Christmas celebrations here are among the most amazing I've witnessed. The park is decorated with glittering lights, enormous Christmas trees, and seasonal garlands, which create a festive ambiance. Christmas Wishes, a heartfelt procession, is one of the highlights. The parade is more than simply the float displays;

it's an immersive experience with renowned Disney characters waving to the audience as traditional holiday music plays.

Special Christmas-themed dining events at The Crystal Palace Restaurant (35.6306° N, 139.8805° E) include seasonal dishes such as roasted turkey and gingerbread desserts. The Christmas mood, mixed with the cuisine, music, and parades, evokes nostalgia and delight in all visitors. It's also a Small World Holiday, a seasonal version of the iconic attraction featuring adorable miniature dolls from across the world dressed in festive costumes. The festive metamorphosis creates a different experience, with cheery melodies and brilliant holiday décor.

Special Events in Tokyo Disneyland
Disney's Easter Celebration

Springtime at Tokyo Disneyland is terrific due to the yearly Easter events. From March to April, the park is decked with pastel-colored decorations and floral arrangements, inspiring feelings of pleasure and regeneration. During this time, you may see the Easter Wonderland Parade, which features lovely Disney characters dressed in bright Easter clothes and participating in a vibrant celebration.

One of the highlights of the Easter season is the Egg Hunt, which takes place at both Tokyo Disneyland and Tokyo DisneySea. This entertaining treasure game challenges visitors to look for hidden Easter eggs throughout the park, which are cleverly themed with Disney characters. It's a terrific family activity that also offers some friendly competition for those wanting something interesting to do in addition to riding.

Anniversary and Themed Celebrations

Tokyo Disneyland enjoys celebrating anniversaries, and the park frequently goes above and beyond during these special anniversary years. For example, the park's 30th-anniversary celebration featured limited-time parades, new shows, and unique goods. Special anniversary performances, such as Dreaming Up! represent the enchantment and memory of Disneyland's past, providing a nostalgic experience for long-time visitors.

Another unique event is the "Duffy & Friends" festival, which honors Tokyo Disneyland's favorite mascot, Duffy, and his buddies. If you come during one of these events, you can anticipate unique Duffy goods, themed attractions, and a unique experience that focuses on Disney's charming and cuddly side.

During these special events, make sure to check the Tokyo Disneyland app for any scheduled performances or showtimes. They sometimes need reservations or specialized viewing areas. The enthusiasm and ingenuity that went into these themed gatherings are worth witnessing personally.

No matter when you visit, Tokyo Disneyland provides an ever-changing and wonderful experience perfectly timed with the seasons. Whether you're watching a Christmas parade, looking for Easter eggs, or commemorating an anniversary, the park's seasonal activities heighten the charm and make each visit feel like a once-in-a-lifetime experience.

STAYING IN TOKYO DISNEYLAND

Staying at Tokyo Disneyland is more than simply a place to relax; it's an essential component of the Disney experience. The lodgings range from colorful Disney hotels to comfortable, budget-friendly alternatives just outside the park, catering to all travelers. I've stayed at a few different homes throughout the park, and I can undoubtedly state that there are plenty of great options, whether you want to immerse yourself in the enchantment or a pleasant place to sleep.

Accommodation Options

Disney Hotels & Resorts

To fully enhance your Tokyo Disneyland experience, staying at one of the Disney Hotels is a no-brainer. These magnificent hotels are more than simply somewhere to stay; they provide an immersive

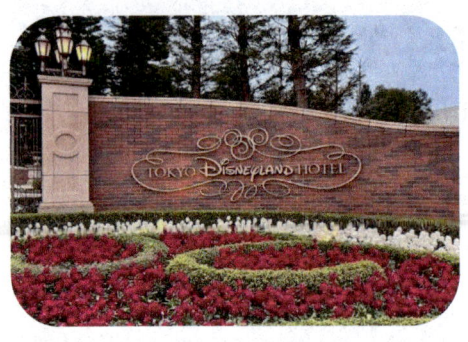

Disney experience that lasts long after you leave the park. I had the pleasure of sleeping at the Tokyo Disneyland Hotel (address: 1-1 Maihama, Urayasu, Chiba 279-8505, Japan; coordinates: 35.6326° N, 139.8815° E), which is located just adjacent to the park entrance.

The Tokyo Disneyland Hotel is a Victorian-style beauty that transports you to a Disney fantasy from the moment you walk in. Every inch of this hotel shouts "magic," from the beautiful rooms furnished with subtle Disney themes to the gorgeous lobby with life-sized statues of popular Disney characters. It is also handy since it is only a short walk from the park gates. And the most significant part? Guests may use the Disney FastPass system, which allows them to avoid lines at some attractions, saving them considerable time.

Another great on-site alternative is the Disney Ambassador Hotel (address: 2-11 Maihama, Urayasu, Chiba 279-0031, Japan; coordinates: 35.6311° N, 139.8847° E). This hotel has a more Art Deco aesthetic, with rooms inspired by classic Disney films. It is equally close to the parks and has amenities similar to the Tokyo Disneyland Hotel but cheaper. These hotels also include Disney character breakfasts, an excellent way to start the day with a touch of Disney enchantment.

Nearby Hotels for Budget Travellers

If you want to avoid staying in the Disney bubble, many alternatives outside the park will keep you near the excitement. **The Hotel Okura Tokyo Bay** (address: 1-8 Maihama, Urayasu, Chiba 279-8585, Japan; coordinates: 35.6284° N, 139.8800° E) is an excellent pick that is only a short monorail ride from the park. While it does not have the same wacky Disney atmosphere, it has oversized accommodations and exceptional service at a lower cost.

For those on an even tighter budget, I recommend checking out the Flexstay Inn Shin-Urayasu (address: 1-3-6 Maihama, Urayasu, Chiba 279-0043, Japan; coordinates: 35.6421° N, 139.8764° E). This modest, no-frills hotel provides modest accommodations at a fair price. It is a little further away from the parks but still easily accessible by train or monorail.

What to Expect at Disney Hotels

Disney hotels are meant to provide a comprehensive experience. Aside from their closeness to the park, they include themed design, excellent facilities, and exceptional customer service. From Disney-themed bedding to special character appearances in the lobby, staying at a Disney hotel is an unforgettable experience. Most hotels have themed rooms with anything from Mickey Mouse wallpaper to subtle nods to Disney classics, so you can feel the enchantment even while you're not at the park.

For example, each room in the Tokyo Disneyland Hotel has a distinct Disney theme, whether it features Cinderella or Peter Pan.

The service is excellent, and your room will have Disney stuff that cannot be found elsewhere. Whether having a character supper or simply meandering around the hotel grounds, there's always something to pique your interest.

Advantages of Staying On-site

Staying on-site at a Disney hotel has several benefits. Not only is the proximity to the park convenient—allowing you to take breaks or return to your accommodation during the day—but you'll also get early park access on certain days, memorable character encounters, and priority bookings for popular activities. The hotel staff is also invaluable in preparing your day at the parks, including maps, showtimes, and food recommendations.

The most significant advantage is the ease of Disney's Magical Express, a specialized shuttle service from the airport to your hotel. It's a peaceful, hassle-free way to begin your Disney vacation without considering transportation.

Tips for Booking Your Stay

Book early to make the most of your stay, especially if you plan to travel during high seasons such as summer or holidays. Disney Hotels are popular; rooms fill quickly, especially during significant events or festivities. Consider scheduling months in advance to get the cheapest rates, and watch for any special deals or bundles.

When booking, look for seasonal activities or holiday-specific incentives that may improve your stay. If you're staying at a Disney hotel, being close to the park is invaluable—especially after a long day of excitement.

Staying at Tokyo Disneyland may take your trip to the next level. Whether you choose the luxury of a Disney hotel or a more affordable option, the park's magic is always just a step away.

TIPS AND RECOMMENDATIONS FOR A SMOOTH VISIT

Many people fantasize about visiting Tokyo Disneyland, but the sheer amount of attractions, parades, and eating options may be intimidating. Over the years, I've discovered a few tactics to help me get the most out of my trips. From avoiding long lineups to making the most of your park experience, here are some vital ideas and advice to make your visit to Tokyo Disneyland as seamless and magical as possible.

Maximising Your Visit
Tips to Avoid Long Lines

Wait times for popular attractions are a regular source of dissatisfaction for visitors to Tokyo Disneyland. Fortunately, you can avoid the worst of the crowd with a bit of preparation. First and foremost, I strongly advise using the Disney FastPass system (now available for certain rides) to bypass the typical waits at key attractions. You may book time for attractions like Space Mountain and Pirates of the Caribbean using the app or at designated FastPass distribution stations.

Another helpful suggestion is to begin with the most popular rides first thing in the morning. Because Tokyo Disneyland opens at 8:00 a.m. (or earlier on busy days), attempt to be at the entrance when it opens to be among the first in line for the big-ticket rides. Popular attractions such as Splash Mountain and Big Thunder Mountain tend to become packed as the day progresses, so visiting them early might save you a lot of time.

The Best Time to Visit and Ride Popular Attractions

When arranging a trip, time is everything. Weekdays are often less crowded than weekends, and if you visit during non-holiday months, you'll have a higher chance of reduced wait times. Additionally, if you want to escape the summer heat, the best seasons are fall and spring, with cooler temperatures and fewer visitors.

For the most incredible experience, I recommend riding thrill rides like Space Mountain or Journey to the Center of the Earth in the mid-afternoon, when many tourists are enjoying a break or attending parades. The lineups for these rides usually are shorter at this time.

Navigating the Park Effectively

Tokyo Disneyland is enormous, and planning your trip ahead of time is essential for getting the most out of your visit. I recommend downloading the Tokyo Disneyland app, which offers real-time information on wait times, restaurant menus, and the park map. It's essential for getting about the park while roaming.

Start your day at Tomorrowland or Adventureland, which are often less busy in the morning. Keep an eye on the map and try to target places near each other. For example, after experiencing Fantasyland, you may travel to Critter Country for the Splash Mountain attraction. This efficient park flow means you only spend a short time strolling from one end to the other.

Essential Packing List
Weather Considerations and What to Wear

The weather in Tokyo may change dramatically depending on the season, so preparing accordingly is critical. Summers may be hot and humid, while winters can be cool, particularly at night. I recommend bringing comfortable shoes (you'll be walking a lot), a light jacket or sweater for chilly evenings, and sun protection (sunscreen, sunglasses, and a hat).

Remember to bring a small portable or misting fan for those going during the summer months to keep calm since the park can become quite hot, especially in busier places. Bringing a small umbrella or rain jacket is always wise if you're visiting in the winter because Tokyo's weather may be unpredictable.

What to Pack for Comfort and Convenience

I recommend taking a portable charger along with your necessities, such as water and food. Because you'll use the Tokyo Disneyland app frequently to monitor wait times and show schedules, ensure your phone is charged. Hand sanitizer and wet wipes are essential for staying clean between rides and meals.

Making the Most of Your Stay
Tips for Eating, Shopping, and Relaxing Between Rides

Tokyo Disneyland has excellent food choices, from themed restaurants to fast-service kiosks. My top pick is the Queen of Hearts Banquet Hall at Fantasyland (address: 1-1 Maihama, Urayasu, Chiba 279-8505, Japan; coordinates: 35.6326° N, 139.8815° E), which serves fanciful Alice in Wonderland-themed cuisine. If you're looking for a snack, try the various popcorn varieties offered around the park, such as curry and chocolate. Eating during off-peak hours, such as late morning or early afternoon, will allow you to avoid massive restaurant queues.

To go shopping, visit the World Bazaar at the entrance. It sells rare Disney products, especially for collectors. It's also an excellent place to get a souvenir to commemorate your experience.

How to Stay Energized and Hydrated All Day

Staying hydrated is essential, especially if you're coming during Tokyo's hot and humid months. Bring a water bottle and use free refills at restaurants and snack vendors. There are lots of energy-boosting foods and drinks available around the park.

Take targeted pauses throughout the day to maximize your productivity. Whether seeing a live concert or getting a bite to eat, having time to relax and recharge can help you prevent tiredness and stay energized for the evening fireworks.

With these pointers, you'll be on your way to a relaxing and delightful trip to Tokyo Disneyland. From making the most of your time in the park to packing wisely, planning early will help you fully enjoy Tokyo Disneyland's wonders.

NEARBY ATTRACTIONS & DAY TRIPS

While Tokyo Disneyland is undeniably magical, the surrounding neighborhood offers much more. Whether you want to prolong your vacation or spice up your Disneyland journey, Tokyo and its surrounding attractions provide plenty of activities for all types of travelers. From renowned sites to gorgeous day outings, here's how to get the most out of your time outside Tokyo Disneyland.

Exploring Tokyo and Beyond

Top Tourist Attractions in Tokyo

Tokyo is a vast metropolis that seamlessly combines tradition and innovation. If you have a day or two, I recommend seeing some of the city's must-see attractions. Begin with Asakusa (address: 2-3-1 Asakusa, Taito City, Tokyo 111-0032; coordinates: 35.7148° N, 139.7967° E), which is home to Japan's oldest and most revered temple, Senso-ji. The lively Nakamise Street leads to the shrine, a treasure trove of traditional delicacies and gifts.

Next, venture into Tokyo's high-energy center with a visit to Shibuya Crossing (address: Shibuya, Tokyo 150-0002; coordinates: 35.6580° N, 139.7016° E), the world's busiest pedestrian crossing. From there, take a trip through Harajuku (address: Jingumae, Shibuya, Tokyo; coordinates: 35.6696° N, 139.7030° E) to view the fashion-forward streets and visit Takeshita Street, which is a must-see for those looking for offbeat stores and excellent crepes.

If you prefer a calmer setting, Meiji Shrine (address: 1-1 Yoyogikamizonocho, Shibuya, Tokyo 151-8557; coordinates: 35.6764° N, 139.6993° E) provides a peaceful respite from the metropolis's hustle and bustle. The calm woodland grounds offer a pleasant escape from Tokyo's hectic pace.

Day Tours to Mount Fuji and Hakone

A day excursion to Mount Fuji and Hakone is highly suggested for those looking for a break from the metropolis. Both sites provide stunning vistas and quiet experiences. Mount Fuji (coordinates: 35.3606° N, 138.7274° E) is Japan's famous emblem. While it may be climbed during the summer, a visit to the Fifth Station offers breathtaking views of the surrounding area. It's an incredible site you won't forget, and it's easily accessible from Tokyo by bus or rail.

For a more leisurely day vacation, consider visiting Hakone (address: Hakone, Kanagawa; coordinates: 35.2323° N, 139.0283° E), a pleasant town noted for its hot springs and scenic lake views. The Hakone Ropeway provides breathtaking views of the mountains and Lake Ashi, and you can take a boat tour on the lake with Mount Fuji towering in the background.

Exploring Disney Resort's Other Parks
DisneySea's Unique Attractions

Beyond Tokyo Disneyland, the Tokyo Disney Resort includes Tokyo DisneySea, a must-see destination for Disney lovers and adventurers. Located just a short distance from Disneyland (address: 1-13 Maihama, Urayasu, Chiba 279-0031; coordinates: 35.6325° N, 139.8804° E), DisneySea is focused on maritime exploration and offers a range of unique attractions not found anywhere else.

Take advantage of Journey to the Center of the Earth, an exciting experience that takes you deep into the Earth's center. Or Indiana Jones Adventure: Temple of the Crystal Skull, a thrilling journey amid ancient ruins. If you're looking for something more peaceful, the scenic Mediterranean Harbor provides breathtaking vistas, and the Venetian Gondola Ride allows you to glide around the park in true Italian style.

Shopping and Dining in Tokyo
Best Shopping Districts in Tokyo

Tokyo is a shopping heaven when you're in the mood to shop. Begin your adventure in the flashy Ginza District (address: Ginza, Chuo City, Tokyo 104-0061; coordinates: 35.6721° N, 139.7655° E), where luxury retailers line the streets. Whether looking for high-end apparel or unique things, Ginza provides an unparalleled shopping experience.

Akihabara (address: Akihabara, Chiyoda City, Tokyo; coordinates: 35.7023° N, 139.7745° E) is a hotspot for electronics, anime products, and unusual devices. Shibuya and Harajuku are great places to get contemporary and one-of-a-kind souvenirs.

Recommended Restaurants and Street Food

After a day of touring or shopping, Tokyo's cuisine culture will leave you plenty of options. **Tsukiji Outer Market** (address: Tsukiji, Chuo City, Tokyo 104-0045; coordinates: 35.6719° N, 139.7701° E) serves the finest sushi and seafood. Dotonbori (address: Dotonbori, Chūō Ward, Osaka 542-0071; coordinates: 34.6686° N, 135.5011° E) serves authentic Japanese comfort cuisine, including takoyaki (octopus balls) and okonomiyaki (savory pancakes).

There are plenty of things to do outside of Tokyo Disneyland, like exploring the city's rich cultural attractions, shopping for souvenirs, and dining at world-class restaurants. A well-rounded trip to the Tokyo region provides an ideal blend of action, leisure, and exploration.

INSIDER TIPS AND PERSONALIZED TRAVEL PLANS

Tokyo Disneyland is a place where dreams come to life in the most enchanting and unexpected ways. Having explored it extensively, I can tell you that the experience here is unlike any other. From the artfully designed attractions to the delightful cuisine, there's so much to enjoy that it can be overwhelming if you don't know where to start. But don't worry—I've got you covered with some insider tips and personalized travel plans that will help you navigate this magical world with ease.

Visitor Reviews and Testimonials

One of the best ways to truly understand the magic of Tokyo Disneyland is through the voices of those who've experienced it. Many visitors share a common sentiment about the park's ability to transport you into another world. A family from Australia, who visited during the spring season, wrote, "Tokyo Disneyland has a charm and energy that's so unique. It's not just about the rides; it's the little details—like the seasonal parades and the impeccably clean streets—that make it so special."

I couldn't agree more. The atmosphere here is one of attention to detail, and this family was right to highlight the charm of the parades. The Dreaming Up! The parade, which runs through the park daily, is a wonderful blend of live music, extravagant costumes, and beloved Disney characters. Another visitor from the UK raved about the immersive experiences at Tokyo DisneySea, saying, "DisneySea feels like a whole new world. The Arabian Coast and Mediterranean Harbor are unlike anything you'll find in the other Disney parks."

For anyone wondering whether the food is worth it, many guests claim it's a major highlight. A group from Canada shared, "The curry-flavoured popcorn and the Gyoza Dog were worth the trip alone!" These popular snacks, found throughout the park, provide a taste of Tokyo Disneyland's unique blend of Western and Japanese influences.

Exclusive Tips from Disney Experts

As someone who's spent countless hours exploring Tokyo Disneyland, I've gathered some key advice from Cast Members and frequent visitors alike that will make your trip more enjoyable and stress-free.

1. Arrive Early and Plan Ahead: If you want to make the most of your day, aim to arrive 30 to 45 minutes before the park opens. Tokyo Disneyland, especially on weekends and holidays, can get crowded quickly. By arriving early, you'll have the chance to head straight for the popular rides like Splash Mountain or Pirates of the Caribbean with shorter wait times.

2. Use the Tokyo Disneyland App: This app is invaluable. It provides up-to-date information on wait times, show schedules, restaurant reservations, and even the locations of all the best restrooms (yes, you'll appreciate this!). It's the easiest way to navigate the park and avoid frustration.

3. **Take Advantage of the FastPass System**: Although it's not as extensive as Disney's FastPass+ in other parks, Tokyo Disneyland offers a similar system that allows you to reserve time slots for certain attractions. For popular rides, this is an absolute must to save time and avoid long waits.

Planning Tips for Solo Travelers

Visiting Tokyo Disneyland solo can be an incredibly rewarding experience. Here's how to make the most of it:

1. **Single-Rider Lines**: Many attractions, including Space Mountain and Big Thunder Mountain, offer single-rider lines, allowing you to skip the regular queues. This is a fantastic perk for solo travellers as it maximizes your time in the park.

2. **Tranquil Spots for Reflection**: While everyone else is rushing to the next big attraction, take some time to enjoy the quieter areas of the park. I found The Enchanted Storybook Castle (35.6329° N, 139.8804° E) to be a peaceful retreat, with its stunning design and less crowded atmosphere. It's the perfect place to sit and take in the beauty of the surroundings.

3. **Solo Dining**: Tokyo Disneyland offers a variety of dining options that are perfect for solo adventurers. One of my favourite places to eat alone is Pan Galactic Pizza Port (34.7550° N, 139.8807° E) in Tomorrowland, where you can enjoy a delicious pizza and watch the world go by. Don't forget to try the Gyoza Dog, a must-have for solo travellers looking to enjoy a snack on the go.

Celebrations and Special Occasions at Tokyo Disneyland

Whether you're celebrating a birthday or anniversary, or just want to mark a special occasion,

Tokyo Disneyland offers plenty of unique ways to do so.

1. Birthday Magic: For a truly magical birthday experience, I recommend stopping by Guest Relations (35.6323° N, 139.8807° E) at the entrance to get a special birthday button. Throughout the day, Cast Members will greet you with "Happy Birthday!"—it's a small touch that makes a big impact.

2. Special Dining Experiences: Consider booking a character dining experience at The Royal Street Veranda (35.6325° N, 139.8806° E), where you can enjoy a delightful meal with beloved Disney characters like Mickey and Minnie. It's the perfect way to celebrate with your favourite Disney friends.

3. Private Tours: For a more exclusive experience, you can book a private tour of the park. These tours include priority access to rides, behind-the-scenes looks at attractions, and a customized itinerary to fit your celebration. It's an unforgettable way to experience Tokyo Disneyland in style.

Personalized Itinerary Suggestions

No two visitors are alike, and Tokyo Disneyland offers something for everyone. Here are a few itinerary suggestions based on your interests:

For Foodies: Start your day at The Hungry Bear Restaurant (35.6335° N, 139.8820° E), known for its hearty Japanese curry. As you explore the park, sample delicious snacks like Popcorn in unique flavours such as soy sauce or honey. For dessert, head to Sweetheart Café (35.6340° N, 139.8796° E) for a refreshing treat.

For Thrill Seekers: If you're an adrenaline junkie, make sure to hit Space Mountain, Big Thunder Mountain, and Splash Mountain early to avoid long wait times. Afterwards, head over to Indiana Jones Adventure: Temple of the Crystal Skull for a thrilling, high-speed ride.

PRACTICAL INFORMATION AND SUSTAINABLE TRAVEL

Tokyo Disneyland is more than just a park—it's an immersive, magical experience. From the lush landscapes to the vibrant parades, there's so much to see and do. As an experienced traveller who has explored this enchanting park extensively, I've gathered some useful insights to help you make the most of your visit while being mindful of your budget, health, and sustainability. Whether you're a first-time visitor or returning for another adventure, these practical tips will guide you through a seamless and memorable experience.

Budget Travel Guide

One of the most common questions I get from fellow travellers is how to enjoy Tokyo Disneyland on a budget. The truth is, with a little planning, it's possible to experience the magic without breaking the bank.

Discounted Tickets: While Tokyo Disneyland offers various ticket options, purchasing your tickets in advance is the best way to save money. You can often find discounted tickets through authorized resellers or the official Tokyo Disneyland website. For example, if you purchase a multi-day pass, the per-day cost is lower compared to buying single tickets.

Food and Snacks: Dining can be expensive at Tokyo Disneyland, but there are ways to save. I found that grabbing a Gyoza Dog (¥650) at the Tomorrowland Terrace (35.6323° N, 139.8807° E) is not only a budget-friendly option but also a delicious one. The park also has affordable meal options like Penny's Pizza (35.6340° N, 139.8805° E) or The Great American Waffle Company (35.6328° N, 139.8820° E), where you can grab tasty quick bites at a reasonable price.

Free Experiences: You don't have to spend money to soak in the magic of Tokyo Disneyland. Take a stroll through the World Bazaar (35.6324° N, 139.8808° E), a stunning shopping street filled with old-timey charm. You can also enjoy the Parades and Seasonal Shows—these are free with park admission and truly embody the heart of the Disney experience. Be sure to grab a spot early for the best view!

Behind the Scenes at Tokyo Disneyland

The magic of Tokyo Disneyland doesn't just lie in its attractions—it's also in the remarkable behind-the-scenes efforts that go into making it all happen. I had the privilege of learning about some of these secrets during my visits.

Attraction Creation: Every attraction at Tokyo Disneyland is meticulously crafted, often with input from the original Disney Imagineers. For example, Pirates of the Caribbean (35.6325° N, 139.8790° E) is renowned for its highly detailed sets and innovative technology. I was amazed to learn that the Tokyo Disneyland version of the ride was adapted to have more dynamic animatronics and immersive sound effects that create a deeper sense of realism.

Seasonal Decorations and Cast Member Training: Seasonal decorations are one of the highlights of Tokyo Disneyland. The park is transformed with each season—from vibrant cherry blossoms in spring to spooky Halloween setups in the fall. What's even more fascinating is how Cast Members receive specialized training to make sure every experience, from costume design to interactions with guests, stays true to Disney's high standards.

Health and Safety Tips

Your health and safety are top priorities during your visit to Tokyo Disneyland. Over the years, I've picked up a few essential tips to ensure a smooth and safe experience.

Accessibility: Tokyo Disneyland is very accommodating to travellers with special needs. The park provides Priority Entrance Passes for guests with disabilities, which allows easier access to rides and attractions. Additionally, wheelchairs and strollers are available for rent at the park entrance (35.6322° N, 139.8809° E).

COVID-19 Precautions: As of my last visit, Tokyo Disneyland has maintained strong health protocols, including regular sanitization of high-touch areas and face mask requirements for guests in certain areas. It's always a good idea to check the latest health updates on the Tokyo Disneyland website before your visit.

Wellness Tips: It's easy to get caught up in the excitement, but don't forget to hydrate! The summer months in Tokyo can be hot and humid, so I recommend carrying a refillable water bottle. There is water fountains scattered throughout the park for refills. Also, take regular breaks in the shaded areas to avoid exhaustion.

Cultural Etiquette for Visiting Tokyo Disneyland

Tokyo Disneyland is a place where cultural appreciation and respect are central. It's important to follow a few local etiquette tips to ensure a pleasant experience for everyone.

Politeness is Key: Japanese culture places a strong emphasis on politeness. Make sure to be respectful to Cast Members and fellow guests. A simple "Arigato" (thank you) goes a long way in showing appreciation for the hard work and effort that goes into creating the magic.

Quiet Spaces and Lines: Japanese guests typically queue up in an orderly fashion, so be sure to follow the lines patiently. Also, while Tokyo Disneyland is an exciting place, it's not as noisy as some of the other parks—Japanese visitors tend to be more subdued, so it's respectful to keep conversations at a low volume.

Photography Etiquette: While it's tempting to snap photos at every corner, be mindful of the rules in certain areas, especially in attractions and dining spots. Always ask for permission before taking photos of other guests, and respect areas where photography is restricted.

Weather Guide and Best Time to Visit

Tokyo Disneyland's weather can vary greatly depending on the time of year, and knowing when to visit can help you avoid crowds and enjoy the park at its best.

Spring (March to May): This is one of the best times to visit. The weather is mild, and the cherry blossoms around the park create a beautiful backdrop. The spring season also brings exciting seasonal events like the Dreaming Up! Parade.

Summer (June to August): While summer can be hot and humid, it's also the time for exciting seasonal events, like Summer Splash. If you don't mind the heat, it's a great time to enjoy water-based attractions like Splash Mountain.

Autumn (September to November): The fall season offers cooler weather and stunning foliage around the park. The Halloween decorations are a highlight, making it a wonderful time to visit.

Winter (December to February): If you enjoy festive decorations and cooler weather, winter is a magical time to visit. Tokyo Disneyland is beautifully decked out for the holidays, and there are fewer crowds compared to other seasons.

Sustainable Travel Tips

Tokyo Disneyland is dedicated to sustainability, and there are several ways visitors can contribute to the park's eco-friendly efforts.

Reduce, Reuse, Recycle: Bring your own reusable water bottle and encourage others to do the same. The park has several recycling bins throughout, so make sure to dispose of your waste properly.

Eco-Friendly Merchandise: Consider purchasing merchandise that supports sustainability, such as eco-friendly bags or reusable products. Many shops offer environmentally conscious options that help reduce waste.

Support Local and Sustainable Dining: Opt for restaurants that prioritize locally sourced ingredients, such as The Grandmother's Kitchen (35.6340° N, 139.8810° E), which features sustainable practices and offers delicious, locally-inspired meals.

Whether you're on a budget, aiming for an eco-friendly trip, or simply seeking practical information, these tips will help you make the most of your visit to Tokyo Disneyland. With a little planning and mindfulness, you can experience the magic of the park in a way that's both enjoyable and sustainable.

Tokyo Disneyland Station Map

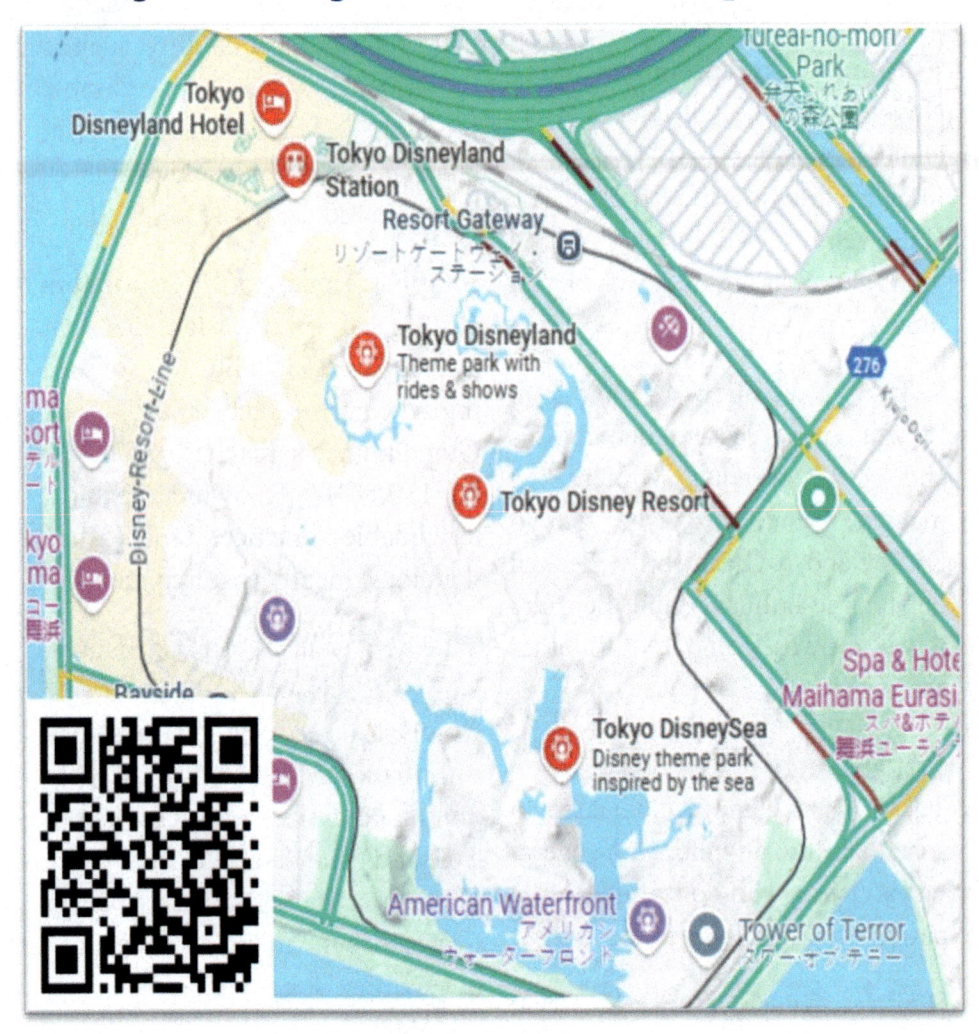

DETAILED MAP AND PHOTOGRAPHY GUIDE

Welcome to your essential guide to discovering and capturing the charm of Tokyo Disneyland. Learn how to utilize QR code maps to navigate the park seamlessly and find the finest photographic sites to create great moments. This chapter mixes practical navigation suggestions with professional photographic advice to help you maximise your Disneyland experience.

How to Use QR Code Maps

Including QR code maps has made it easier to navigate Tokyo Disneyland than ever before. Upon entering the park, visitors may download the official Tokyo Disneyland app, which includes interactive maps accessible via QR codes strategically placed throughout the park. Here's how to make use of these digital maps:

Scan the QR Code: Look for QR codes at strategic locations such as entrances, main attractions, and dining places. Scan the code with your smartphone's camera or a QR code scanner app, and the interactive map within the Tokyo Disneyland app will appear immediately.

Interactive Features: The interactive map displays real-time information on attraction wait times, show schedules, and food options. Users may sort attractions by kind, height requirements, or popularity to help them organize their days more efficiently.

Personalized Itineraries: Use the map's itinerary builder to organize your day according to your preferences. You may save favourite destinations, create reminders for parades and shows, and get updates on local events or special discounts.

Accessible Options: The QR code maps provide accessible features for guests with special needs. Filter sites are equipped with accessibility features such as wheelchair-friendly pathways, accessible restrooms, and help services to guarantee a pleasant visit for all.

Language Support: The app supports many languages, allowing foreign guests to traverse the park with ease. Switch between Japanese, English, Chinese, and other languages to get maps and information in your favourite language.

Augmented Reality (AR) Integration: Some QR code maps include AR capabilities, which create an immersive experience. Point your phone's camera at select sites to reveal more information, amusing facts, and hidden mysteries around Tokyo Disneyland.

Visitors may enhance their Tokyo Disneyland experience by using QR code maps, which provide efficient navigation, personalized planning, and interactive elements to ensure a memorable and stress-free visit.

Best Places for Photography

Tokyo Disneyland is a photographer's paradise, with breathtaking vistas, renowned monuments, and colourful characters. Consider these excellent photography sites to create unforgettable memories:

Cinderella Castle: The showpiece of Tokyo Disneyland, Cinderella Castle is an excellent backdrop for photographs. Visit after sunrise or sunset to capture the best photos of the castle. Nighttime photographs with the castle illuminated and pyrotechnics in the backdrop are equally stunning.

World Bazaar: The lovely, brick-lined World Bazaar district provides picturesque landscapes with its old architecture and festive decorations. Capture the sense of Disney enchantment with images of Main Street, U.S.A., which is busy with visitors and covered with seasonal decorations.

Fantasyland Gardens: This location is ideal for flowery and whimsical photos. The gardens' vivid hues, mixed with fairy-tale constructions such as Alice's Tea Party and Peter Pan's Flight, make a magical environment for unforgettable images.

Tomorrowland's Star Wars Launch Bay: For Star Wars lovers, the Star Wars Launch Bay in Tomorrowland is a must-see attraction. Photograph legendary figures like Darth Vader and BB-8 against the exhibit's future environment to add a sense of adventure to your gallery.

Toontown: The fun and colourful Toontown area is excellent for spontaneous photos with your favourite Disney characters. From Mickey's House to Roger Rabbit's Car Toon Spin, the vivid backdrops offer several options for fun and exciting images.

Enchanted Tiki Room and Adventureland: These themed sections provide distinct and exotic surroundings. Capture the lush vegetation and tropical feelings of Adventureland, or the wonderful atmosphere of the Enchanted Tiki Room, where flora and wildlife come to life.

Seasonal Decorations and Parades: Tokyo Disneyland is well-known for its beautiful seasonal decorations and parades. Whether it's the bright lights of Halloween, the glistening snow of Christmas, or the vibrant colours of spring festivals, these occasions provide dramatic and entertaining photo possibilities.

Hidden Gems & Unique Perspectives: Discover lesser-known locations such as the tranquil vistas from the park's bridges, the fine features of themed facades, and lofty vantage points for panoramic photographs of the whole park. These hidden jewels frequently provide the most distinctive and intimate photos.

Nighttime Illuminations & Fireworks: As the day fades to night, Tokyo Disneyland transforms into a dazzling fantasy. Capture the wonderful glow of lighting attractions, reflections in water features, and the spectacular fireworks display that illuminates the night sky.

Character Meet and Greets: Use character meet and greet areas to take photographs with your favourite Disney characters. Whether it's a candid moment or a prepared photograph, these interactions bring a personal and delightful element to your photo collection.

By visiting these popular photographic locations and organizing your photos around the park's wonderful surroundings and happenings, you can create a spectacular visual diary of your Tokyo Disneyland journey.

Tokyo Disneyland ATMs Map

Tokyo Disneyland Things to Do

Restaurants Map

Tokyo DisneySea

Tokyo Disneyland Pharmacies

Tokyo Bay Maihama Hotel First Resort

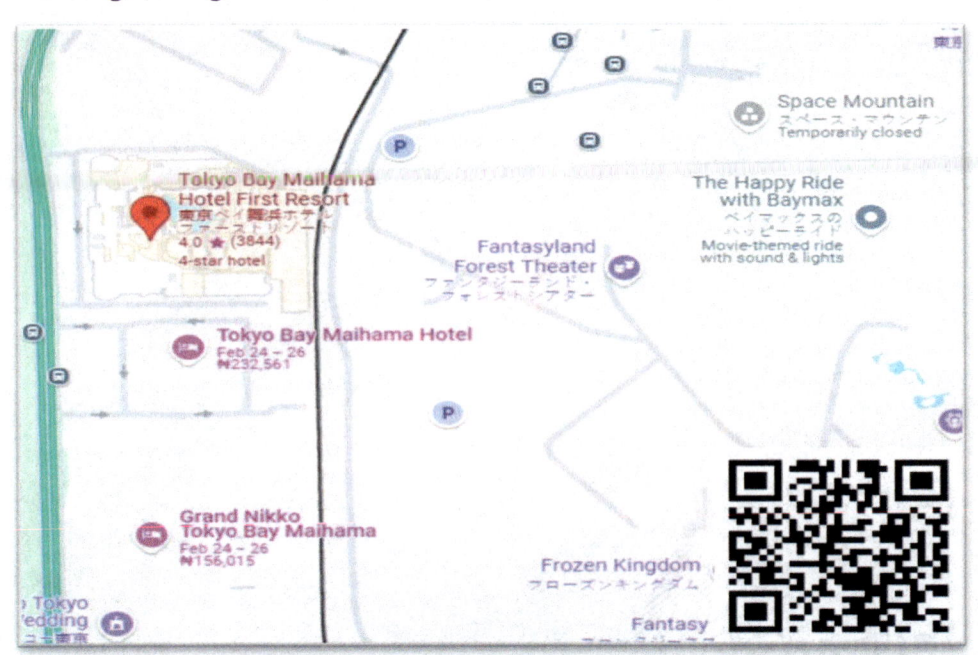

Tokyo Disneyland Hotel

APPENDIX

Useful Apps for Tokyo Disneyland

When visiting Tokyo Disneyland, a few applications might make your trip easier and more fun. I recommend installing these practical applications ahead of time:

Tokyo Disneyland App

This official app (available for iOS and Android) is an excellent resource. It displays real-time wait times for rides, meal reservations, and entertainment. You can also use it to map the park and receive directions, making travel simple. It also allows you to purchase Disney FastPasses and view event schedules.

Google Maps

Navigating Tokyo may be difficult for first-timers, but Google Maps is essential for directions and public transit recommendations. It also gives real-time walking and transit instructions to and from the park, making it easy to explore the surroundings.

HyperDia

HyperDia helps organize journeys across Tokyo and beyond, particularly when taking public transit. This program lets you plan train routes, travel times, and costs for journeys to Tokyo Disneyland, the city center, and day trip locations like Mount Fuji and Hakone.

Yelp Japan

Yelp is great for discovering the best restaurants, cafés, and other eateries in and near the Disneyland Resort. Whether looking for a quick snack or a complete dining experience, Yelp's user ratings can help you find the best locations.

Useful Websites

The official Tokyo Disneyland website provides complete park information, event calendars, and ticket sales. It is routinely updated with park news, discounts, and recommendations to provide a flawless experience.
https://www.tokyodisneyresort.jp/en/

Japanese National Tourism Organization (JNTO)

The Japan National Tourism Organization's website provides extensive travel information on Japan, including top attractions, travel ideas, and practical guidance.
https://www.japan.travel/en/

HyperDia (For transportation)

The HyperDia website assists you in planning your travels throughout Tokyo and Japan, including getting to Tokyo Disneyland from various locations in the city.
https://www.hyperdia.com/

Emergency Contacts

While Tokyo is a generally secure city, it's always important to know the emergency numbers just in case:

Emergency Services (Police, Ambulance, and Fire) - 110 (Police) and 119 (Fire and Ambulance)

Tokyo Disneyland Lost and Found: +81 47-305-4444

Tokyo Tourist Information Center (general inquiries): +81 3-5321-3070

Embassy of Your Country (for Foreign Nationals in Case of Emergency)—Contact information varies, so make sure to preserve the phone number for your country's embassy in Japan before you travel.

FAQs

Q: When is the best time of year to visit Tokyo Disneyland?

A: The best time to visit is during the off-peak seasons, generally spring (March to May) and fall (September to November). These months skip the peak summer months and Japanese festivals like Golden Week. If you want to avoid crowds and enjoy the weather, try going on weekdays outside of peak seasons.

Q: Do I need to purchase tickets in advance?

A: Yes, especially at busy times. Tickets may be purchased online through the official Tokyo Disneyland website or from approved agents. Purchasing in advance secures entrance and helps you to arrange your day more effectively.

Q: How can I make a dinner reservation?

A: Dining reservations may be made using the Tokyo Disneyland app or the official website. You should book reservations soon, especially at famous themed restaurants.

Q: Are there any discounts for kids or seniors?

A: Tokyo Disneyland provides cheap tickets for children (ages 4-11) and seniors (60 and up). Check the official website for the most recent prices and discounts.

Q: What is the easiest method to travel to Tokyo Disneyland from Tokyo Station?

A: Take the JR Keiyo or JR Musashino Line to Maihama Station (approximately 15-20 minutes) from Tokyo Station. From there, it's a short walk to the park gate.

With this handy appendix, you now have all the tools and information you need to organize a flawless and wonderful vacation to Tokyo Disneyland! Safe travels, and enjoy the magic!

CONCLUSION

Tokyo Disneyland is unlike any other place, combining Disney's enchantment with Japan's rich culture to create a memorable experience. Whether you're a first-time visitor or a long-time Disney fan, the park has diverse activities, entertainment, and eating options to suit all ages and interests. From the whimsical appeal of vintage rides to the heart-pounding thrills of the most recent attractions, Tokyo Disneyland is where memories are built and dreams are realized.

As you tour the park, take advantage of the hidden jewels, seasonal events, and themed experiences that give Tokyo Disneyland its personality. The meticulous attention to detail, superb service, and seamless integration of traditional Disney enchantment with Japanese hospitality create an atmosphere where guests feel welcome and immersed in a world of joy.

Plan ahead of time and take advantage of the numerous tools available to get the most out of your stay. Whether you download the Tokyo Disneyland app, use FastPass, or follow the helpful advice in this book, there is no reason why your visit to the park won't be seamless and pleasurable. When you're ready to leave the park, the dynamic metropolis of Tokyo and its surroundings provide many choices for exploration, from retail districts to tranquil temples to breathtaking day excursions.

Ultimately, Tokyo Disneyland is more than simply a theme park; it's a celebration of pleasure, creativity, and the power of narrative. Prepare for an experience filled with laughter, amazement, and lifelong memories.

Glossary of Terms

A system that allows people to book access to specific attractions, minimizing wait times by enabling them to return at a set time to ride the ride.

Character Meet & Greets

There are unique locations where guests may meet, photograph, and engage with their favorite Disney characters.

Themed Areas

Tomorrowland, Fantasyland, and Adventureland are three distinct areas of the park meant to transport guests to various worlds.

Duffy, the Disney Bear

A renowned Disney character specific to the parks, he was noted for his cute look and various related items and events.

DisneySea is a distinctive portion of the Tokyo Disney Resort that offers nautical-themed attractions and a separate experience from the classic Disneyland park.

Disney parades and performances run through designated places in the park, showcasing characters, floats, and music.

The MagicBand is a wearable gadget at Disney parks that allows access to FastPass, will enable you to make payments, and opens hotel room doors.

Ride Restraints

Lap bars, seat belts, and shoulder harnesses are safety measures to keep passengers secure at various attractions.

Cast Members
The word describes Disney personnel taught to give excellent client service and bring Disney's enchantment to life.

Disney Dining Plan
A prepaid meal package that allows guests to purchase meals in advance of their visit to the park, providing flexibility and potential savings.

Imagineering
A portmanteau that combines the words "imagination" with "engineering," referring to the creative process of designing Disney attractions and experiences.

Themed Dining: Restaurants throughout the park are created to match the ambiance of a given region or film, providing unique culinary experiences.

E-Ticket Attractions
The park's most popular and exciting rides are often reserved for the most expensive ticket attractions.

Annual Pass
A form of ticket that permits repeat visitors to enter the park at a discounted fee all year.

Crowd Calendars anticipate predicted crowds on certain days, allowing tourists to schedule their visit during less congested periods.

Disney Villages are outdoor shopping and eating areas near resorts or entrances that provide Disney products and themed food options.

Themed merchandise
Souvenirs are explicitly developed for park themes, attractions, characters, or seasonal events.

Single Rider Line
A line of tourists is eager to ride alone to fill vacant seats on rides and shorten wait times.

Seasonal events
The park hosts special events and festivals throughout the year, including Halloween, Christmas, and New Year's Eve.

Park Hopper
A ticket option that permits tourists to visit various parks within the Tokyo Disney Resort (such as Disneyland and DisneySea) on the same day.

Notes

Notes

Printed in Great Britain
by Amazon